# NEAR-DEATH EXPERIENCES

Near-death experiences and its explanation in Neuropsychology

Nandikaa

pencil

ISBN 978-93-5667-940-5
© Nandikaa 2023

Published in India 2023 by Pencil

*A brand of*
One Point Six Technologies Pvt. Ltd.
Unit no. 26, Ground Floor, Building A1,
Wadala Truck Terminal Road,
Near Post Office, Antop Hill, Mumbai - 400037
**E** connect@thepencilapp.com
**W** www.thepencilapp.com

*All rights reserved worldwide*

No part of this publication may be reproduced, stored in or introduced into a retrieval system, or transmitted, in any form, or by any means (electronic, mechanical, photocopying, recording, or otherwise), without the prior written permission of the Publisher. Any person who commits an unauthorized act in relation to this publication can be liable to criminal prosecution and civil claims for damages.

DISCLAIMER: *The opinions expressed in this book are those of the authors and do not purport to reflect the views of the Publisher.*

# Author biography

Nandika Kapani a student in highschool student. Currently researching Neuropsychology and various phenomena related to it.

A passionate student who wants to change the world for the better by providing improvement in modern Neuropsychology.

# CONTENTS

Chapter 1 The Phenomenon of Near-Death Experiences .............................................................. 5

# Chapter 1 The Phenomenon of Near-Death Experiences

Imagine getting into an accident and suddenly you are on an otherworldly journey, filled with vivid imagery, feelings of peace, and encounters with a realm beyond our physical existence. Well it is true, many people who have undergone such unconscious experiences, have stated that they were in a "different world". The Mysteries of the human mind are both awe-inspiring and puzzling. Welcome to the captivity world of neuropsychology.

**Near-death experiences [NDE] are one of the most puzzling phenomena in psychology. NDE has challenged our understanding of consciousness, life, and death. "where do we go when we are unconsciousness?" have been the most prying concern for everyone. Here, we will unravel the mysteries of NDE and its role in Neuropsychology.**

Chapter 1: The Phenomenon of Near-Death Experiences Near-death experiences (NDEs) have fascinated humanity for centuries, going beyond cultural, religious, and geographical boundaries. In this chapter, we will understand the phenomenon of NDE and explore its historical, cultural, and cross-culture aspects. By examining

NDEs' diverse perspectives and interpretations, we aim to lay the foundation for a deeper understanding of this extraordinary phenomenon. In examining the historical perspectives of near-death experiences, we uncover a tapestry of beliefs and accounts that date back centuries. Throughout different cultures and civilizations, encounters resembling NDEs have been documented and interpreted within the context of their respective times.

Ancient Egyptian Mythology: In ancient Egypt, the belief in an afterlife and the journey of the soul played a significant role. The Book of the Dead, a collection of funerary texts, describes the soul's journey through the underworld, encountering various challenges and judgments similar to the elements found in modern NDE accounts.

The ancient Egyptians believed in the existence of the Duat, a realm associated with the afterlife and the journey of the soul. It was believed that upon death, the soul would embark on a perilous journey through the Duat, encountering various challenges and judgments.

One crucial element in Egyptian mythology related to the afterlife is the "Weighing of the Heart" ceremony. According to the Book of the Dead and other funerary texts, the heart of the deceased would be weighed against the feather of Ma'at, the goddess of truth and justice. This process represented a judgment of the individual's deeds and moral character during their earthly life.

During the journey through the Duat, the soul would encounter various deities, guardians, and gatekeepers. These encounters resembled the encounters with beings reported in modern NDE narratives. Some of these entities would provide guidance, protection, or judgment to the soul as it progressed through the afterlife realm.

At the culmination of the journey, the soul would reach the Hall of Two Truths. Here, the deceased would make declarations of innocence and truthfulness before a tribunal of gods, including Osiris, the god of the afterlife. The soul's fate and the possibility of attaining eternal life would depend on the outcome of this judgment.

While ancient Egyptian mythology did not explicitly describe near-death experiences as they are understood today, the concepts of a perilous journey through the afterlife encounters with deities and guardians, and a judgment of one's deeds and character resonate with elements found in contemporary NDE accounts. These beliefs provided the ancient Egyptians with a framework for understanding the transition from life to the afterlife and the potential for transformation and eternal existence.

Greek Mythology: In Greek mythology, the story of Orpheus, who descended into the underworld to retrieve his beloved Eurydice, shares similarities with NDE narratives. The concept of crossing a threshold between life and death, encountering otherworldly beings, and returning with newfound wisdom resonates with elements found in contemporary NDE reports.

The story of Orpheus, a legendary musician and poet, descending into the underworld to retrieve his beloved Eurydice, shares similarities with NDE narratives. Orpheus crosses the boundary between life and death, encounters otherworldly beings, and experiences a profound journey through the realm of the dead. His quest to return from the realm of the deceased echoes the themes of transcending death and the desire to reunite with loved ones that resonate within NDE accounts.

The myth of Persephone, who was abducted by Hades and became the queen of the underworld, is associated with the ancient Greek religious ritual known as the Eleusinian Mysteries. Initiates into these mysteries were believed to undergo a transformative experience involving a symbolic journey through death and rebirth. The details of the rituals are not entirely known, but the initiates' experience of descending into darkness and emerging with a newfound understanding mirrors the transformative elements of NDEs.

Greek mythology also includes descriptions of different realms associated with the afterlife. The Elysian Fields, a paradise-like realm, and Tartarus, a place of punishment, are among the realms mentioned in various myths. These realms can be seen as symbolic representations of different types of post-death experiences, reminiscent of the diverse encounters reported in NDE narratives.

Numerous Greek myths involve encounters between mortals and divine beings or deceased souls. These interactions often occur in dreams or altered states of consciousness, during which the mortal temporarily enters a realm beyond the ordinary. These encounters parallel the encounters with spiritual beings or deceased loved ones reported in NDE accounts.

While Greek mythology does not provide a direct account of NDEs as they are understood today, its stories and themes touch upon aspects of the transcendent experiences described by individuals who have undergone NDEs. These myths reflect the ancient Greeks' contemplation of life, death, and the potential for extraordinary journeys beyond the physical realm.

Near-Death Experiences in Literature: In literature, we

find references to NDE-like experiences. In Dante Alighieri's Divine Comedy, the protagonist embarks on a journey through Hell, Purgatory, and Heaven, providing vivid descriptions of otherworldly realms and encounters with souls. Such literary works serve as a testament to the enduring fascination with transcendent experiences throughout history.

Dante's epic poem takes readers on a journey through Hell (Inferno), Purgatory (Purgatorio), and Heaven (Paradiso). Dante's protagonist travels through these realms, encountering souls and divine beings. His voyage shares similarities with NDE accounts, as he moves through different planes of existence and gains insight into the nature of the divine and the human condition.

In this beloved holiday classic, Ebenezer Scrooge undergoes a transformative experience when visited by three spirits. Through encounters with these apparitions, Scrooge confronts his past, present, and future, gaining a renewed perspective on his life. This NDE-like encounter catalyzes Scrooge's redemption and a reflection on the choices that shape one's existence.

Although not explicitly an NDE, Abbott's novella explores the concept of consciousness transcending dimensions. The protagonist, a two-dimensional being, encounters a sphere from a higher-dimensional realm, allowing him to perceive realities beyond his limited perspective. This encounter prompts a profound shift in his understanding of the universe and parallels the transformative nature of NDEs.

Albom's novel follows the journey of Eddie, an elderly maintenance worker who dies and enters the afterlife. In a series of encounters with five individuals, Eddie gains insight into the interconnectedness of lives and the impact of his actions. This exploration of the afterlife and the lessons learned through encounters with deceased individuals echoes themes often found in NDE narratives.

These literary works demonstrate how authors have used near-death experiences as powerful storytelling devices to explore existential questions, personal growth, and the mysteries of life and death. Through these narratives, readers are invited to contemplate the transformative potential of such encounters and the profound impact they can have on individuals' perspectives and choices.

Modern Accounts and Scientific Exploration: While historical perspectives offer insights into cultural interpretations of NDE-like experiences, it was not until the 20th century that scientific investigations began to shed light on the phenomenon. The publication of Raymond Moody's book "Life After Life" in 1975 sparked increased interest in the subject and encouraged scientific inquiry into NDEs, leading to subsequent research and exploration.

Raymond Moody's book "Life After Life," published in 1975, is often credited with popularizing the term "near-death experience" and bringing attention to the phenomenon. Moody conducted interviews with individuals who had reported NDEs, identifying common themes such as out-of-body experiences, encountering a light, and a sense of peace. His work sparked widespread interest and further research into NDEs.

Researchers have collected and analyzed numerous accounts of NDEs to identify common features and patterns. Through surveys, interviews, and questionnaires, scientists have documented recurring elements such as the sensation of leaving the body, moving through a tunnel, encountering deceased loved ones or spiritual beings, and experiencing a life review. These data have helped establish a foundation for understanding the subjective experiences associated with NDEs.

Scientific investigations have also explored the underlying neurobiological and psychological mechanisms that may contribute to NDEs. Neuroimaging studies have examined brain activity during NDE-like experiences, highlighting areas such as the temporal lobes, frontal cortex, and limbic system. Psychological factors, including the role of beliefs, emotions, and cognitive processes, have also been studied to better understand the subjective nature of NDEs.

One intriguing aspect of NDEs is the occurrence of veridical perceptions—accurate observations made by individuals during their NDEs that are later confirmed to be true. These include details of events or objects that were not accessible to their physical senses during the experience. Researchers have conducted investigations to validate these claims, contributing to the growing body of evidence supporting the authenticity of NDEs.

Studies have examined the long-term effects of NDEs on individuals' beliefs, attitudes, and well-being. Many people report profound and positive transformations following their NDEs, including a greater appreciation for life, a decreased fear of death, increased compassion, and a deeper sense of purpose. Research has explored the potential psychological and existential implications of NDEs and their impact on individuals' lives.

Scientific exploration of NDEs faces challenges, including the subjective nature of the experiences, the lack of standardized definitions, and the potential for confounding factors. Skeptics have proposed alternative explanations, such as physiological, psychological, or cultural factors, to account for the subjective experiences reported during NDEs. These alternative explanations continue to be debated within scientific circles.

Modern accounts and scientific exploration of near-death experiences have provided valuable insights into this complex phenomenon. Through rigorous research and interdisciplinary investigations, scientists have contributed to our understanding of the subjective experiences, potential mechanisms, and impacts associated with NDEs. However, many questions remain, and ongoing research continues to deepen our understanding of the mysteries surrounding near-death experiences.

Cultural Variations

NDEs transcend cultural boundaries, yet they manifest in unique ways within different societies. In this section, we will explore the cultural variations in near-death experiences, examining how factors such as religious beliefs, societal norms, and individual perspectives influence the interpretation and expression of these encounters. By recognizing the cultural nuances, we gain a deeper appreciation of the diversity and universal aspects of NDEs.

Cultural and Religious Beliefs: Cultural and religious beliefs strongly influence how individuals interpret and describe their near-death experiences. For example, in Western cultures influenced by Christianity, individuals may report encounters with angels or religious figures. In contrast, in cultures with strong beliefs in reincarnation, NDEs may be interpreted as glimpses into the afterlife or the realm between lives.

In Christian cultures, NDEs are often interpreted within the framework of Christian beliefs about the afterlife. Individuals may report encounters with religious figures such as angels, Jesus, or departed loved ones. The presence of a bright light or a tunnel may be seen as symbolic of the pathway to heaven or God's presence.

In Islamic cultures, NDEs are viewed through the lens of Islamic teachings. Some Muslims report encounters with divine beings or the Prophet Muhammad during their NDEs. The experience may be seen as a spiritual journey or a test of faith, and individuals may interpret it within the context of Islamic beliefs about the soul's journey after death.

Hinduism, with its beliefs in reincarnation and karma, influences the interpretation of NDEs in Hindu cultures. NDEs may be seen as glimpses into the afterlife or the realm between lives. The life review aspect of NDEs may be interpreted as an assessment of one's actions and their karmic consequences.

In Buddhist cultures, NDEs may be understood in terms of the Buddhist concepts of impermanence and rebirth. Individuals may interpret their experiences as glimpses into different realms of existence or as opportunities for spiritual growth and liberation from the cycle of rebirth.

Indigenous cultures often have unique interpretations of NDEs rooted in their traditional beliefs and practices. NDEs may be seen as encounters with ancestral spirits, journeys to other dimensions, or experiences that provide guidance and healing. The interpretation of NDEs varies greatly among different indigenous cultures around the world.

In secular societies, individuals may interpret NDEs

outside of religious or spiritual frameworks. The experiences may be seen as neurological or psychological phenomena, emphasizing scientific or psychological explanations rather than spiritual or metaphysical ones.

Symbolism and Imagery: The symbols, imagery, and cultural references used to describe NDEs can vary across different cultures. For instance, individuals from Western cultures might describe a tunnel or a bright light during their NDEs, while individuals from other cultures may use different symbols and metaphors to represent their experiences. Cultural symbols, such as sacred rivers or mythical creatures, may also appear in NDE accounts.

The image of a tunnel is frequently mentioned in NDE narratives. Individuals often describe traveling through a tunnel with a bright light at the end. The tunnel represents a transitional space between life and the afterlife or a realm beyond ordinary consciousness.

The presence of bright light is a pervasive symbol in NDEs. The light is often described as warm, radiant, and inviting. It represents a divine or spiritual presence, symbolizing enlightenment, love, and guidance. The light may also convey a sense of peace, comfort, and transcendence.

During NDEs, individuals commonly report a sense of leaving their physical bodies and observing their surroundings from an external perspective. This out-of-body experience is often depicted as looking down upon one's own body or hovering above it. The OBE symbolizes a detachment from physical limitations and the potential separation of consciousness from the physical form.

Encounters with deceased loved ones are frequently

reported in NDEs. These encounters symbolize a reunion with departed family members or friends and often convey a sense of love, comfort, and reassurance. Seeing and interacting with deceased loved ones provides a powerful emotional and spiritual connection.

The life review is a prominent element in many NDEs, where individuals report a panoramic review of their life events and actions. This review often emphasizes the impact of one's choices and their consequences on oneself and others. It symbolizes reflection, self-evaluation, and the opportunity for growth and understanding.

In some cases, individuals report encountering symbols or imagery specific to their native culture or religious background. For example, individuals with Native American heritage might describe encountering sacred animals or natural elements, while those with religious backgrounds may report encounters with religious figures or symbols specific to their faith.

Interpretation of Life Review: Life review, a common element of NDEs, is the process where individuals re-experience important moments of their lives. The way individuals interpret and understand this aspect of their NDE can vary across cultures. Some cultures might view the life review as a moral judgment, an opportunity for self-reflection, or a chance to reconcile past actions, while others might interpret it in different ways based on their cultural and religious beliefs.

The life review offers individuals the opportunity to reflect upon their actions, decisions, and their impact on themselves and others. It is often described as a non-judgmental process where individuals experience a compassionate and unbiased assessment of their life. The purpose of this reflection is to gain insight, understanding, and a deeper awareness of one's thoughts, emotions, and behaviors.

During the life review, individuals often report experiencing the emotions and perspectives of the people they interacted with throughout their lives. This empathic understanding allows individuals to gain a profound sense of the consequences of their actions on others. It fosters compassion, forgiveness, and the recognition of interconnectedness, promoting a greater understanding of the effects of one's behavior on the well-being of others.

The life review is frequently described as a transformative experience, where individuals gain profound insights and lessons from their past actions. They may realize the importance of love, kindness, and positive contributions to others. Individuals often report a renewed focus on personal growth, spiritual development, and the desire to make amends or live in alignment with higher principles.

The life review can provide individuals with a sense of purpose and clarity about their life's meaning and direction. It helps them evaluate whether they have fulfilled their life's purpose or if there are areas they need to focus on or improve upon. The life review can motivate individuals to make changes in their lives, pursue new goals, and prioritize what truly matters to them.

It's important to note that interpretations of the life review may vary based on individual beliefs, cultural background, and personal experiences. Some individuals may perceive the life review as a divine judgment or as a psychological phenomenon related to memory retrieval and processing. Others may view it as an opportunity for personal growth, reconciliation, or spiritual evolution.

Afterlife Concepts: Cultural beliefs about the afterlife influence how NDEs are understood and integrated into individuals' worldviews. Some cultures envision the afterlife as a specific place or realm, while others view it as a continuation of earthly existence or a reunion with ancestors. These cultural variations shape the narratives and explanations individuals provide for their NDEs.

Many individuals describe their NDEs as glimpses of a heavenly realm or paradise. This concept is often associated with religious beliefs that envision a place of peace, beauty, and eternal happiness. Individuals may report encountering divine beings, angels, or departed loved ones in these heavenly realms.

In NDEs, some individuals report experiences that suggest the possibility of reincarnation. They may describe meeting deceased relatives or encountering other beings who guide them through the process of choosing or planning their next life. These experiences align with belief systems that emphasize the cycle of birth, death, and rebirth.

NDEs often involve encounters with realms or dimensions that individuals interpret as spiritual or transcendent. These realms may be perceived as beyond the physical world and associated with a sense of expanded consciousness, higher knowledge, and interconnectedness. Some individuals describe these experiences as a reunion with a divine source or a merging with a universal consciousness.

Certain NDE accounts suggest a continuity of life after death. Individuals may report a sense of still being alive or existing in a different form beyond the physical body. They may describe engaging in activities, interacting with other beings, or having a sense of purpose or mission in this continued existence.

Some NDEs involve experiences that are interpreted as moments of judgment or life assessment. Individuals may report feeling a review of their actions, thoughts, and intentions, often accompanied by a deep sense of self-awareness and understanding. This assessment can be perceived as an evaluation of one's moral or spiritual progress.

Social and Community Impact: The social and community impact of NDEs can differ across cultures. In some cultures, NDEs may be openly discussed and accepted, and individuals may receive support and validation from their communities. In contrast, in cultures where NDEs are not widely understood or accepted, individuals may face skepticism or even rejection when sharing their experiences.

NDEs often reinforce or deepen individuals' belief in an afterlife or spiritual realm. These experiences can provide individuals with a firsthand encounter with the possibility of life beyond death. This increased belief in an afterlife can have a profound impact on an individual's spirituality, religious practices, and worldview.

NDEs frequently lead to personal transformations, as individuals often report a renewed sense of purpose, meaning, and a shift in values. They may prioritize relationships, love, and compassion, and develop a greater appreciation for life and its preciousness. These changes can extend beyond the individual and positively impact their relationships and interactions within their communities.

NDEs often evoke a profound sense of interconnectedness and unity among individuals. Those who have had similar experiences may form support networks or communities to share and discuss their experiences. These communities can provide validation, understanding, and a sense of belonging for individuals who may feel isolated or struggle to integrate their experiences into their everyday lives.

NDEs can have a significant emotional and psychological impact on individuals. Some individuals may experience a sense of awe, wonder, or profound peace following their NDE. However, others may face challenges such as difficulty integrating the experience into their sense of self, confusion, or existential questioning. Support from loved ones, mental health professionals, or NDE support groups can be crucial in navigating the emotional and psychological aspects of NDEs.

NDEs often challenge cultural taboos and fears surrounding death and dying. Individuals who have had NDEs may develop more open and accepting attitudes toward death, viewing it as a transition rather than an endpoint. This can influence end-of-life care, hospice practices, and discussions about death within communities.

NDEs have sparked scientific and academic interest, leading to research and studies on the phenomenon. The exploration of NDEs contributes to the fields of psychology, neuroscience, consciousness studies, and philosophy. This research can have an impact on medical and psychological practices, end-of-life care, and our understanding of human consciousness.

Common Features

Despite the cultural variations, near-death experiences often share common features. In this section, we will delve into the core elements that define NDEs, including the sensation of leaving the body, moving through a tunnel or to a different realm, encountering deceased loved ones or spiritual beings, and experiencing a sense of peace, love, and a life review. By exploring these common threads, we can identify the fundamental aspects that unite diverse NDE accounts.

Out-of-Body Experience (OBE): Many individuals report a sense of detachment from their physical bodies during an NDE. They may describe observing their bodies from an external perspective or floating above them. This out-of-body experience is often accompanied by a feeling of lightness or freedom.

During an OBE, individuals often report observing their physical bodies from a vantage point outside of themselves. They may describe seeing their own body lying on a hospital bed, floating above it, or looking down at it from a higher position. This external perspective provides a sense of detachment from the physical body.

People who have experienced OBEs in NDEs often report a heightened state of awareness and perception. They describe having a clearer and more vivid perception of their surroundings than what is typically experienced in their normal waking state. Some individuals even report being able to see and hear things that were outside the range of their normal physical senses.

During an OBE, individuals often describe a sense of freedom of movement and the ability to navigate through their environment without the constraints of the physical body. They may move effortlessly, float, or glide through walls and other solid objects. This freedom of movement adds to the feeling of liberation and detachment from the physical realm.

In some cases, individuals who have an OBE during an NDE report being able to interact with the physical environment. They may touch objects, manipulate them, or communicate with people in the vicinity. However, the level of interaction can vary, and some individuals may feel more limited in their ability to influence the physical world. OBEs in NDEs often evoke strong emotions in individuals. They may experience a mixture of awe, wonder, excitement, or fear during the out-of-body experience. The profound nature of the OBE can leave a lasting emotional impression on individuals, influencing their beliefs and perceptions about the nature of consciousness and reality.

Tunnel: A significant number of individuals describe traveling through a tunnel during their NDE. The tunnel is often described as having a bright light at the end, drawing the person towards it. The tunnel experience is often associated with a feeling of peace and a transition from the earthly realm to another dimension.

During an NDE, individuals often describe the sensation of entering or being drawn into a tunnel. The tunnel is typically described as a passageway or a pathway that appears to extend into the distance. The tunnel is often described as dark or dimly lit, with a sense of narrowing or convergence towards a brighter light at the end.

While in the tunnel, individuals report a sense of movement or being propelled forward. This movement can vary in speed and intensity. Some individuals describe a rapid or accelerated movement, while others perceive a more gentle or gradual progression. The sensation of movement is often described as effortless and smooth.

As individuals travel through the tunnel, they often report

changes in their perception. The environment may appear different from the physical world, with altered colors, heightened clarity, or a sense of vibrancy. Some individuals describe a feeling of being surrounded by a loving or comforting presence during this journey.

The tunnel experience is often interpreted as a transition from the earthly realm to another dimension or state of existence. It is seen as a symbolic passage from life to death, from the physical to the spiritual realm. Individuals may feel a sense of leaving behind their earthly attachments and entering into a different state of consciousness or reality.

One of the significant aspects of the tunnel experience is the presence of bright light at the end of the tunnel. This light is often described as intense, radiant, and inviting. Individuals may experience a sense of warmth, love, and peace emanating from the light. Many interpret this light as a representation of a divine or spiritual presence.

Intense Emotions: During an NDE, individuals often experience intense emotions, such as profound peace, love, joy, or a sense of being unconditionally accepted. These positive emotions are frequently described as more intense and blissful than any experienced in earthly life.

Many individuals describe a profound sense of peace and serenity during their NDEs. This peace is often described as far beyond any peaceful experience they have had in their earthly lives. It is a deep, all-encompassing calmness that transcends any worries, fears, or anxieties.

Individuals frequently report feeling an overwhelming sense of unconditional love during their NDEs. This love is often described as pure, all-embracing, and non-judgmental. It is a love that transcends human limitations and is often associated with a divine or spiritual presence.

NDEs often evoke feelings of intense bliss and joy. Individuals describe experiencing a state of unparalleled happiness and ecstasy that surpasses any earthly pleasures. This joy is often accompanied by a sense of freedom, lightness, and a deep appreciation for the beauty and wonder of existence.

Some individuals report having mystical or transcendent experiences during their NDEs. They may describe feeling a profound connection to something greater than themselves, such as a universal consciousness or divine presence. This connection can evoke emotions of awe, wonder, and a deep sense of reverence.

Many individuals who have had NDEs express an overwhelming sense of gratitude for life and the opportunity to experience existence. They may feel a deep appreciation for their loved ones, the beauty of the world, and the interconnectedness of all things. This gratitude often leads to a shift in priorities and a renewed zest for life.

While positive emotions are commonly reported in NDEs, some individuals also experience moments of fear, anxiety, or confusion. These emotions can arise during the initial stages of the NDE, especially when individuals are confronted with the unfamiliar and the unknown. However, these negative emotions are often replaced by positive emotions as the NDE progresses.

Encounter with Beings of Light: Many individuals report encountering beings of light or spiritual entities during their NDEs. These beings are often described as radiant, loving, and wise. They may be interpreted as deceased loved ones, religious figures, or unidentified entities that convey a sense of guidance, support, and unconditional love.

During an NDE, individuals often report encounters with beings of light. These beings are described as emanating a radiant, glowing light that is perceived as pure, loving, and compassionate. The light is often described as brighter and more intense than any light experienced in the physical world.

The beings of light are commonly associated with an overwhelming sense of unconditional love and acceptance. Individuals who encounter these beings often describe feeling embraced and enveloped in a profound love that transcends any human experience. This love is described as all-encompassing, non-judgmental, and infused with a deep sense of compassion.

Communication with beings of light in NDEs often transcends conventional spoken language. Individuals report a telepathic or intuitive form of communication, where thoughts, emotions, and concepts are exchanged instantaneously. This form of communication is described as being filled with profound wisdom, understanding, and guidance.

Encounters with beings of light in NDEs are frequently described as transformative and enlightening. These beings are often perceived as wise, knowledgeable, and spiritually advanced. They may provide insights, guidance, or answers to the individual's questions. The wisdom shared by these beings can have a profound impact on the individual's understanding of life, purpose, and the nature of reality.

The interpretation of these beings varies across cultural and personal beliefs. Some individuals may interpret them as deceased loved ones, angels, spiritual guides, or divine entities. Others may see them as representations of higher consciousness or aspects of their own deeper self. The interpretation is often influenced by the individual's religious, spiritual, or cultural background.

Encounters with beings of light often bring a deep sense of comfort, reassurance, and peace to individuals during their NDEs. The presence of these beings is described as calming, soothing, and supportive. They may offer a sense of protection and guidance, helping individuals navigate the unfamiliar and sometimes overwhelming aspects of the NDE.

Sense of Transcendence: Individuals often describe a sense of transcending time, space, and physical limitations during an NDE. They may report experiencing a higher level of consciousness, expanded awareness, or a merging with a universal or divine presence. This sense of transcendence can be accompanied by a feeling of interconnectedness with all things.

Many individuals who have had NDEs describe an expanded or heightened state of awareness. They report a sense of perceiving and understanding reality beyond the limitations of their physical senses. This expanded awareness often includes a broader perspective, enhanced clarity of thought, and a deeper understanding of life's mysteries.

A sense of transcendence in NDEs often involves a profound connection to a universal or divine presence. Individuals may describe feeling connected to a higher power, a cosmic consciousness, or a collective energy. This connection is often experienced as a deep sense of unity, interconnection, and oneness with all things.

During an NDE, individuals frequently report merging or becoming one with a radiant light or energy. This merging is often described as a dissolution of boundaries between the self and the surrounding universe. It can evoke a profound sense of peace, love, and a feeling of being enveloped in a higher, transcendent reality.

A sense of transcendence in NDEs is often accompanied by a loss of conventional notions of time and space. Individuals may describe a sense of timelessness, where past, present, and future merge into a single eternal moment. Similarly, the concept of physical space may dissolve, with individuals perceiving a boundless, infinite expanse.

Transcendence in NDEs can involve mystical and spiritual encounters. Individuals may report encounters with deceased loved ones, religious or spiritual figures, or beings of light. These encounters often convey profound insights, guidance, and a sense of divine presence. The mystical experiences in NDEs can be deeply transformative and have a lasting impact on the individual's beliefs and worldview.

The sense of transcendence in NDEs often expands an individual's consciousness beyond their ordinary state. They may gain a deeper understanding of the interconnectedness of all things, the purpose of life, and the nature of reality. This expanded consciousness can lead to a profound shift in the individual's values, priorities, and beliefs about the meaning of existence.

Return to the Body: In many NDE accounts, individuals describe a point at which they have to choose to return to their physical bodies or continue their journey into the afterlife. Some individuals report being reluctant to return, while others feel compelled to do so, often with a renewed sense of purpose.

During an NDE, individuals may suddenly become aware that they need to return to their physical bodies. This awareness can be accompanied by a sense of urgency or a feeling that their time in the NDE realm is coming to an end. They may realize that unfinished tasks or responsibilities are awaiting them in the physical world.

Upon returning to the body, individuals often describe a process of reconnection. They may feel a sense of merging or integration as their consciousness re-establishes a connection with their physical form. This reconnection can be accompanied by sensations of heaviness, pressure, or a feeling of "snapping" back into the body.

As individuals return to their bodies, they typically regain their sensory and physical perception. They become aware of their surroundings, including the sounds, sights, and physical sensations associated with their physical body and the immediate environment. This transition from the NDE realm to the physical realm can involve a readjustment period.

After returning to the body, individuals may retain memories of their NDE. These memories can vary in clarity and intensity, with some individuals having detailed recollections and others experiencing fragmented or symbolic memories. The integration of the NDE experiences into their ongoing life can be a gradual process, and individuals may need time to make sense of the profound and transformative nature of their NDE.

The return to the body in NDEs often brings about significant life changes for individuals. They may undergo a shift in perspective, priorities, and beliefs as a result of their NDE experiences. The integration of the NDE into their daily life can involve a reassessment of relationships, and career choices, and a deepening of spiritual or existential understanding.

Life-Changing Transformations:

NDEs are often described as deeply transformative experiences that profoundly impact individuals' lives. In this section, we will examine the long-lasting effects of NDEs on individuals' beliefs, values, and priorities. We will explore the psychological, emotional, and spiritual transformations that occur following these experiences, shedding light on their potential to enhance well-being, increase compassion, and foster a deeper connection to the mysteries of existence.

Shift in Perspective: After an NDE, individuals often experience a significant shift in their perspective on life and death. They may gain a deeper understanding of the interconnectedness of all beings, the purpose and meaning of life, and the transient nature of physical existence. This shift in perspective often leads to a greater appreciation for life and a desire to live more authentically and purposefully.

One of the fundamental changes in perspective reported in NDEs is an expanded awareness of reality. Individuals may describe a heightened sense of consciousness, clarity, and understanding that surpasses their normal state of awareness. They may perceive a broader, interconnected nature of existence and gain insights into the nature of reality.

During an NDE, individuals often transcend the limitations of their physical body and experience a sense of freedom and liberation. This can lead to a shift in perspective regarding the nature of identity and the temporary nature of physical existence. They may come to view the physical body as a vessel for consciousness, rather than the core of their being.

NDEs frequently lead to a profound belief in the continuity of consciousness beyond death. Individuals may report experiencing a timeless, eternal aspect of themselves that transcends the boundaries of physical life. This belief in an ongoing existence beyond death can have a transformative effect on their perspective on life, death, and the purpose of human existence.

NDEs often bring a deep sense of interconnectedness and unity with all living beings and the universe as a whole. Individuals may describe a profound understanding that everything is interconnected and that separation is an illusion. This perspective can foster feelings of compassion, empathy, and a sense of responsibility towards others and the environment.

Following an NDE, individuals often experience a reevaluation of their values and priorities in life. They may place greater importance on love, kindness, compassion, and personal growth. Materialistic pursuits and external achievements may become less significant, while relationships, inner fulfillment, and making a positive impact on others and the world may take precedence.

NDEs often bring a heightened appreciation for the present moment and a deepened sense of gratitude for life. Individuals may develop a greater awareness of the beauty and preciousness of everyday experiences. They may strive to live more mindfully, fully embracing each moment and finding joy in the simple aspects of life.

Reduced Fear of Death: Many individuals who have had NDEs report a reduction in their fear of death. Through their NDE experiences, they often gain a sense of the continuity of consciousness beyond the physical body and a belief in the existence of an afterlife. This newfound understanding can bring comfort and peace, allowing individuals to approach death with less anxiety and fear.

During an NDE, individuals may have a direct experience of continuity of consciousness beyond the physical body. They may report feelings of peace, serenity, and even bliss during the NDE, which can provide a firsthand glimpse of an existence beyond death. This direct experience can alleviate the fear of the unknown that is often associated with death.

Many individuals who have had NDEs describe encountering a loving and accepting presence during their experience. This presence, often described as a divine being, a higher power, or deceased loved ones, emanates a sense of unconditional love and acceptance. The encounter with this presence can instill a deep sense of reassurance, leading to a decreased fear of death.

During an NDE, individuals may experience a sense of detachment from physical pain and suffering. They often report feeling a profound sense of peace, well-being, and freedom from the limitations of their physical body. This transcendence of physical suffering can provide a glimpse into a state of existence where pain and fear are no longer present, reducing the fear of death as a source of pain and suffering.

NDEs can shift the perception of death from being an absolute end to a transition or a continuation of consciousness in a different form. Individuals may come to view death as a natural part of the human journey, akin to passing from one state of existence to another. This understanding can alleviate the fear of death by framing it as a process rather than an ultimate end.

The transformative nature of NDEs often leads to a reassessment of beliefs and a broader worldview. Individuals may develop a belief in an afterlife, a higher power, or a spiritual reality beyond the physical realm. These beliefs can provide a sense of meaning, purpose, and comfort, reducing the fear of death as they believe in the continuity of existence beyond the physical body.

NDEs often bring a heightened awareness of the present moment and an appreciation for the preciousness of life. This focus on the present can lead to a shift in perspective, where individuals prioritize living fully and embracing each moment rather than fixating on the fear of eventual death.

Spiritual Awakening: NDEs frequently trigger profound spiritual awakenings in individuals. They may experience a deep connection to a higher power, universal consciousness, or divine presence. This spiritual awakening can lead to a renewed sense of faith, a deepening of religious beliefs, or the exploration of new spiritual paths. Individuals may also develop a greater interest in spiritual practices, such as meditation, prayer, or contemplation.

During an NDE, individuals often experience an expanded state of consciousness that goes beyond their everyday awareness. They may have a heightened sense of clarity, perception, and connection to a greater reality. This expanded awareness can lead to a deep spiritual awakening, where individuals feel a profound connection to something beyond their physical existence.

NDEs frequently involve encounters with a higher power, divine beings, or a loving and benevolent presence. Individuals may describe feeling embraced by unconditional love, acceptance, and guidance. These encounters can awaken a deep sense of spirituality, as individuals feel connected to a higher power or divine presence that transcends their understanding of the physical world.

Following an NDE, individuals often undergo a profound transformation of their beliefs and values. They may experience a shift in religious or spiritual beliefs or explore new spiritual paths. The NDE can challenge preexisting notions of God, the afterlife, and the purpose of life, leading to a more expansive and inclusive worldview. This transformation often involves a deepened sense of connection, compassion, and reverence for all life.

NDEs often lead to a profound experience of oneness and interconnectedness with all beings and the universe. Individuals may describe a deep understanding that we are all interconnected, part of a greater whole, and inseparable from each other and the divine. This sense of oneness can awaken a spiritual consciousness that transcends individual identity and fosters a deep sense of compassion and unity.

After an NDE, individuals often feel compelled to engage in spiritual practices such as meditation, prayer, contemplation, or mindfulness. These practices can deepen their connection to the spiritual realm and help integrate their NDE experiences into their daily lives. Spiritual practices provide a way to nurture awakened spiritual awareness and maintain a sense of connection to the divine.

Spiritual awakening in NDEs often leads to a heightened sense of purpose and a desire to be of service to others. Individuals may feel a calling to contribute positively to the world, guided by a deepened understanding of the interconnectedness of all life. This sense of purpose can inspire individuals to make meaningful changes in their lives and actively participate in the betterment of humanity. Increased Empathy and Compassion: Following an NDE, individuals often report a heightened sense of empathy and compassion towards others. They may feel a deeper understanding of the challenges and struggles that people face in life and a greater desire to help and support others. This increased empathy can lead to more caring and altruistic behaviors, as well as a shift in values towards kindness, love, and acceptance.

During an NDE, individuals may experience a heightened sense of interconnectedness with all beings. This expanded awareness allows them to have a deeper understanding of the challenges, emotions, and experiences faced by others. They may gain insights into the interconnected nature of human suffering and develop a greater capacity to empathize with the struggles of others.

NDEs frequently involve encounters with a loving and accepting presence or a divine being. This encounter often elicits a profound experience of unconditional love and acceptance. Individuals may internalize this experience and extend that love and acceptance to others, fostering empathy and compassion as they recognize the inherent worth and value of all individuals.

Following an NDE, individuals often undergo a reevaluation of their priorities and values. Material possessions, status, and external achievements may become less significant, while empathy, kindness, and compassion take on greater importance. This shift in values can lead to a greater focus on the well-being and happiness of others, inspiring acts of compassion and service.

NDEs can increase individuals' sensitivity to the suffering of others. Having experienced a state of love, peace, and oneness during the NDE, individuals may be more attuned to the pain and struggles of others. This heightened sensitivity motivates them to alleviate suffering and offer support and comfort to those in need.

Many individuals who have had NDEs feel a strong desire to make a positive impact on the world. They may feel a sense of responsibility to use their renewed perspective and understanding to contribute to the well-being of others. This can manifest in various forms, such as engaging in acts of kindness, volunteering, or advocating for social justice causes.

NDEs often bring about a profound sense of forgiveness and understanding. Individuals may experience a release of past resentments, grudges, and judgments, realizing the interconnectedness and shared humanity of all individuals. This cultivation of forgiveness and understanding fosters compassion towards oneself and others, leading to more empathetic and forgiving attitudes.

Healing and Transformation: NDEs can bring about profound healing and transformation on emotional, psychological, and even physical levels. Individuals may experience a release of past traumas, resentments, and negative emotions, leading to emotional healing and a newfound sense of inner peace. They may also report improvements in their overall well-being, including a reduction in anxiety, depression, and physical ailments.

In some cases, individuals who have had an NDE report experiencing spontaneous physical healing. They may recover from illnesses, injuries, or chronic conditions following their NDE. This healing can be attributed to the profound energetic and spiritual shifts that occur during the NDE, which can have a positive impact on the physical body.

NDEs often bring about deep emotional and psychological healing. Individuals may experience a release of fear, anxiety, and emotional burdens they were carrying before the NDE. They may gain insights into the root causes of their emotional struggles and find healing through the experience of unconditional love, forgiveness, and acceptance during the NDE.

NDEs can facilitate the release of deep-seated traumas and negative patterns that were affecting individuals' lives. The transformative nature of the NDE allows individuals to gain a new perspective on their past experiences and find healing through forgiveness, understanding, and self-compassion. This release of trauma can lead to a profound sense of liberation and freedom.

NDEs often trigger a deep spiritual transformation in individuals. They may experience a profound shift in their beliefs, understanding of the nature of reality, and connection to the divine. This spiritual transformation can lead to a sense of inner peace, purpose, and a deepened connection to oneself and others.

Following an NDE, individuals often undergo a reevaluation of their values and priorities in life. Materialistic pursuits and external achievements may become less important, while relationships, personal growth, and making a positive impact on others may take precedence. This shift in values can lead to a more fulfilling and purposeful life.

NDEs often bring about a profound sense of self-love and self-acceptance. Individuals may experience a deep understanding of their inherent worth and value as spiritual beings. This newfound self-love and acceptance can have transformative effects on their self-esteem, relationships, and overall well-being.

After an NDE, individuals often seek to integrate the insights and experiences from their NDE into their daily lives. They may strive to live in alignment with the newfound understanding of love, compassion, and interconnectedness they gained during the NDE. This integration can lead to positive changes in their relationships, careers, and overall lifestyle.

Shift in Priorities: Many individuals who have had NDEs undergo a significant reevaluation of their priorities in life. They may place less importance on material possessions, status, and external achievements, and instead prioritize experiences, relationships, personal growth, and making a positive impact on others. This shift in priorities often leads to a more fulfilling and meaningful life.

Following an NDE, individuals often place a greater emphasis on nurturing and deepening their relationships with loved ones and the people around them. They may prioritize spending quality time with family and friends, expressing love and appreciation, and fostering meaningful connections. The experience of love and interconnectedness during the NDE can inspire a desire for more authentic and fulfilling relationships.

NDEs frequently trigger a deepened interest in personal growth and spiritual development. Individuals may embark on a journey of self-discovery, seeking to understand themselves on a deeper level and explore their spiritual nature. They may engage in practices such as meditation, mindfulness, or studying spiritual texts to foster their personal and spiritual growth.

After an NDE, individuals often reevaluate their values and align their actions with what truly matters to them. Materialistic pursuits and external achievements may take a back seat to live a life of integrity, compassion, and authenticity. They may prioritize living in alignment with their core values, making choices that reflect their true beliefs and principles.

NDEs frequently inspire individuals to make a positive impact on the world and contribute to the well-being of others. They may feel a deep sense of purpose and a calling to help alleviate suffering, promote kindness, and create positive change. This can manifest in various forms, such as volunteering, advocacy, or engaging in acts of kindness and compassion.

NDEs often bring about a heightened appreciation for the present moment and the beauty of everyday life. Individuals may develop a greater awareness of the preciousness of time and the fleeting nature of existence. They may strive to live more mindfully, fully embracing the present moment and finding joy in simple experiences.

Following an NDE, individuals may experience a shift in their relationship with material possessions and attachments. They may recognize the impermanence of worldly possessions and place less importance on accumulating wealth or material goods. Instead, they may focus on cultivating inner richness, and finding joy in experiences and relationships rather than material accumulation.

NDEs often awaken a sense of curiosity and a desire for exploration and new experiences. Individuals may feel a renewed zest for life and a willingness to step outside of their comfort zones. They may seek out opportunities for personal growth, travel, learning, and embracing new challenges as part of their expanded perspective on life.

Skepticism and Debates:

Given the profound nature of near-death experiences, skepticism and debates have naturally emerged. In this section, we will explore the critical viewpoints and scientific skepticism surrounding NDEs. We will discuss alternative explanations, such as physiological and psychological factors, and the challenges in studying and validating these experiences. By acknowledging different perspectives, we encourage a balanced and nuanced understanding of the phenomenon.

Scientific Explanations: Skeptics often seek to provide scientific explanations for NDEs that do not involve the existence of a transcendent or spiritual realm. They may attribute NDEs to physiological or psychological factors, such as oxygen deprivation, hallucinations, neurochemical processes, or the activation of specific brain regions. These explanations focus on the idea that NDEs can be understood solely within the framework of the physical body and brain.

Neurobiological explanations focus on the role of the brain in generating NDEs. They suggest that various physiological and neurochemical processes contribute to the subjective experience. For example, researchers have proposed that oxygen deprivation, such as during cardiac arrest, can trigger altered states of consciousness, including vivid sensory experiences, feelings of peace, and hallucinations.

Studies using neuroimaging techniques, such as functional magnetic resonance imaging (fMRI), have identified specific brain regions that are activated during NDEs. Some researchers suggest that the activation of these regions, such as the temporal lobe or the limbic system, may contribute to the visual, emotional, and memory components of NDEs.

Psychological and cognitive explanations emphasize the role of psychological and cognitive processes in shaping NDEs. They propose that the experience may arise from a combination of factors, including memory recall, altered perception of time, the activation of emotional centers in the brain, and the influence of personal beliefs, cultural expectations, and prior knowledge.

NDEs share similarities with dream-like states and hallucinatory experiences. Some researchers propose that NDEs may be similar to lucid dreaming, where individuals are aware that they are dreaming and have a sense of control over the experience. Others suggest that NDEs may be akin to drug-induced hallucinations or other altered states of consciousness.

NDEs often occur during moments of extreme stress or trauma, such as cardiac arrest or life-threatening situations. Researchers speculate that the experience may be a coping mechanism or a defense mechanism of the brain, helping individuals process and make sense of the overwhelming situation. The release of endorphins and other stress-related neurochemicals may also contribute to the subjective experience of peace and well-being.

Cultural and social factors can shape the interpretation and content of NDEs. Researchers suggest that the cultural and religious beliefs of individuals may influence the specific imagery, symbols, or encounters reported during NDEs. Social and environmental factors may also play a role in how NDEs are perceived and interpreted by individuals and their communities.

Interpretation and Subjectivity: Debates surrounding NDEs often revolve around the interpretation and subjective nature of the experiences. Skeptics may argue that NDEs are primarily influenced by cultural, religious, or personal beliefs, suggesting that their content is shaped by preexisting expectations or cultural narratives. They emphasize the need for careful analysis and consideration of alternative explanations for the reported phenomena.

NDEs are highly personal experiences, and individuals interpret them based on their own beliefs, values, and cultural backgrounds. The interpretation of NDEs can vary widely, with some individuals attributing the experience to a spiritual or transcendent realm, while others may explain it through psychological or physiological factors. Personal interpretation influences how individuals make sense of the experience and integrate it into their worldview.

Cultural and religious beliefs play a significant role in shaping the interpretation of NDEs. Different cultures and religions have unique frameworks and narratives to understand life, death, and the afterlife. Individuals may interpret their NDEs within the context of their cultural or religious beliefs, resulting in variations in the content, symbols, and encounters reported during the experience.

Cultural and religious influences also influence how NDEs are perceived and understood within different societies. Individuals' preexisting beliefs and expectations can shape their interpretation of NDEs. For example, individuals who hold strong religious beliefs may interpret their NDEs as confirmation of their religious teachings or the existence of an afterlife. On the other hand, skeptics or individuals with a materialistic worldview may interpret NDEs as purely physiological or psychological phenomena. The interpretation of NDEs can be influenced by confirmation biases, where individuals seek to confirm their existing beliefs or expectations.

NDEs often involve rich symbolism and profound meaning for the experiencers. Symbols such as tunnels, light, life reviews, or encounters with deceased loved ones may carry personal significance and deep emotional impact. The interpretation of these symbols and the overall meaning of the NDE experience can vary among individuals, reflecting their unique personal histories, values, and life circumstances.

The subjective interpretation of NDEs affects how individuals integrate these experiences into their lives and sense of identity. NDEs can be transformative, prompting individuals to reevaluate their values, priorities, and beliefs. The subjective interpretation of the experience influences whether individuals view it as a source of personal growth, spiritual awakening, or a reaffirmation of their worldview.

NDEs can vary in terms of their content, intensity, and overall experience. Some individuals report pleasant and uplifting experiences, while others describe distressing or confusing episodes. The interpretation of NDEs is influenced by the specific details and emotional impact of the experience. Different interpretations can arise even from seemingly similar NDEs due to the subjective nature of perception and memory.

Lack of Empirical Evidence: Critics of NDEs often highlight the limited empirical evidence and methodological challenges associated with studying these experiences. They question the reliability and validity of anecdotal accounts and emphasize the need for rigorous scientific investigation through controlled experiments, brain imaging studies, or longitudinal studies. Skeptics argue that the current body of research on NDEs falls short of providing conclusive evidence for their existence or the existence of an afterlife.

NDEs are deeply personal and subjective experiences, making them challenging to study using traditional scientific methods. They rely on self-reported accounts and memories, which can be influenced by various factors such as biases, memory distortions, and individual interpretation. Anecdotal evidence, though valuable for understanding the subjective experience, is often considered insufficient in establishing broader scientific claims.

Studying NDEs presents several methodological challenges. The unpredictability of NDE occurrences makes it difficult to conduct controlled experiments or systematically gather data. Ethical considerations also limit the ability to induce near-death situations in research settings. Additionally, the retrospective nature of most studies relying on self-reporting introduces potential recall bias and challenges in verifying the accuracy of reported experiences.

NDEs are highly diverse and can vary in content, intensity, and cultural context. This variability makes it challenging to establish standardized criteria for identifying and studying NDEs. The lack of consensus on defining NDEs and their specific characteristics hampers efforts to collect consistent empirical data across studies and establish a solid foundation of evidence.

Reproducing and validating NDE experiences under controlled conditions is difficult. Researchers face limitations in reproducing the unique combination of physiological, psychological, and environmental factors that contribute to NDEs. Replicating individual experiences reported during NDEs, such as encounters with deceased loved ones or spiritual beings, poses significant challenges and may rely heavily on personal belief systems.

Studies exploring NDEs often face challenges in obtaining large and diverse samples due to the relatively rare occurrence of NDEs and the difficulty in recruiting participants who have experienced them. Small sample sizes limit the statistical power of studies and make it challenging to generalize findings to broader populations. Additionally, the inclusion of individuals with varying cultural and religious backgrounds is important for capturing the full spectrum of NDE experiences.

Psychological and Neurological Perspectives: Skepticism regarding NDEs often draws upon psychological and neurological perspectives. Critics propose that NDEs can be understood as a product of the mind's capacity to generate vivid and complex experiences during periods of altered brain functioning. They explore how the brain's neurochemistry and neural networks may contribute to the various elements reported in NDEs, such as the tunnel experience, encounters with beings, or life reviews.

Psychological perspectives suggest that NDEs may be a unique form of altered state of consciousness. They propose that during life-threatening situations, the brain undergoes physiological and neurochemical changes, leading to shifts in perception, self-awareness, and cognitive functioning. NDEs share similarities with other altered states, such as meditation, psychedelic experiences, or certain types of dreaming.

NDEs often occur in situations of extreme stress, such as cardiac arrest or traumatic events. From a psychological perspective, NDEs can be seen as adaptive coping mechanisms or defense mechanisms employed by the mind to manage the overwhelming situation. They may provide comfort, a sense of control, or a way to make meaning out of the experience.

Memory plays a crucial role in shaping the content and interpretation of NDEs. Psychological perspectives propose that NDEs may involve the activation of memory recall processes. This can include the retrieval of autobiographical memories, emotional memories, or fragmented memories from various life events. The consolidation and integration of these memories during or after the NDE can contribute to the richness of the experience.

Neurological perspectives explore the role of neurochemical and neurobiological processes in the occurrence of NDEs. Some researchers suggest that the release of endogenous opioids, serotonin, or other neurotransmitters during a life-threatening situation can modulate neural activity and contribute to the vivid visual imagery, feelings of peace or euphoria, and altered time perception reported in NDEs.

Neuroimaging studies have provided insights into the brain mechanisms underlying NDEs. Functional magnetic resonance imaging (fMRI) and electroencephalography (EEG) studies have shown specific patterns of brain activation during NDEs. For example, certain brain regions, such as the prefrontal cortex, temporal lobes, or limbic system, may exhibit altered activity, connectivity, or synchronization. These brain changes may be associated with the reported experiences, including the sense of floating, encounters with deceased loved ones, or life reviews.

Psychological perspectives emphasize the influence of personal beliefs, cultural expectations, and prior knowledge on the interpretation of NDEs. Individuals' preexisting beliefs and expectations may shape the content and meaning ascribed to their NDEs. For example, cultural and religious beliefs can influence the interpretation of encounters with beings of light or deceased loved ones.

Cultural and Individual Variations: Debates also center around the cultural and individual variations in NDEs. Skeptics argue that the content and interpretation of NDEs can be influenced by cultural and individual factors, suggesting that the experiences are not universally consistent. They emphasize the need for cross-cultural studies and a deeper understanding of the cultural, social, and psychological influences on NDE narratives.

Cultural factors play a significant role in shaping the interpretation and expression of NDEs. Different cultures have distinct beliefs, values, and religious frameworks that influence how NDEs are perceived and understood.

Cultural expectations and religious teachings may provide a lens through which individuals interpret their NDEs. For example, the presence of specific religious figures or symbols in NDEs may reflect the cultural and religious backgrounds of the individuals.

Religious beliefs and spiritual traditions heavily influence the interpretation of NDEs. Individuals with religious backgrounds may interpret their experiences within the framework of their religious teachings, such as concepts of heaven, hell, or reincarnation. The religious and spiritual interpretations of NDEs can vary widely across different faiths and belief systems, leading to diverse descriptions and understandings of the phenomenon.

The symbolic content and imagery reported in NDEs can vary based on cultural and individual factors. Symbolic elements may be influenced by cultural icons, mythology, or personal experiences. For instance, encounters with deceased loved ones or spiritual beings may take different forms and have different meanings across cultures. Cultural symbolism and individual beliefs can shape the interpretation and significance of these encounters.

The cultural and linguistic context also affects how individuals describe and communicate their NDEs. Language may influence the choice of words, metaphors, and expressions used to convey the experience. Different cultures may have specific terminology or conceptual frameworks for discussing NDEs, and individuals may adapt their descriptions to fit within their cultural norms and linguistic capabilities.

Individual variation is inherent in NDEs, as each person brings unique life experiences, beliefs, and psychological makeup to their interpretation of the experience. Personal values, fears, and expectations shape the individual's understanding of the NDE. Two individuals experiencing similar NDEs may interpret and describe them differently based on their subjective perceptions, memories, and cognitive processes.

Individual and cultural variations in emotional and psychological factors can influence the interpretation of NDEs. For example, the emotional impact of the experience, such as feelings of peace, love, or fear, may vary among individuals. Psychological factors such as personality traits, coping mechanisms, and prior trauma can also influence the individual's interpretation and integration of the NDE into their lives.

Methodological Challenges and Bias: Critics of NDEs point out methodological challenges in studying the phenomenon, such as recall bias, subjective interpretation of experiences, and the lack of standardized research protocols. They argue that these challenges may introduce confounding factors and limit the reliability of research findings, calling for more rigorous methodologies and controls to address these limitations.

NDE research often relies on self-reported accounts from individuals who have experienced an NDE. This can introduce selection bias, as individuals who choose to share their experiences may have unique characteristics or motivations that differ from those who do not report their NDEs. This bias can affect the generalizability of findings to the broader population and may limit the understanding of NDEs.

NDEs are often retrospectively reported, which introduces the potential for recall bias. The memory of the NDE experience may be influenced by factors such as the passage of time, subsequent life events, personal beliefs, and cultural influences. Memory distortions and gaps can impact the accuracy and consistency of reported NDE accounts, making it challenging to establish a precise understanding of the experiences.

Cultural and interpretive bias can influence the way individuals interpret and describe their NDEs. Cultural factors, such as religious beliefs and cultural expectations, can shape the content and meaning attributed to NDEs. Similarly, personal beliefs, preconceived notions, and individual interpretations can introduce bias into the reporting and interpretation of NDEs. Researchers must be mindful of these biases and consider them when analyzing and interpreting the data

Defining and identifying NDEs using standardized criteria can be challenging due to the diverse nature of the experiences reported. The absence of universally accepted criteria for classifying and categorizing NDEs can lead to inconsistencies in research methodologies and findings. The lack of a standardized approach hampers efforts to compare and synthesize results across studies.

Obtaining large and diverse samples of individuals who have experienced NDEs can be difficult due to the relatively rare occurrence of these experiences and the challenges associated with recruitment. Small sample sizes limit the statistical power of studies and may make it challenging to draw robust conclusions or generalize findings to broader populations.

Replicating NDEs in controlled experimental settings is challenging due to ethical considerations and the unpredictable nature of NDE occurrences. The inability to reproduce the exact conditions under which NDEs occur limits the ability to validate and replicate reported experiences. Replication studies are crucial for establishing the reliability and validity of findings in NDE research.

Social and reporting biases can influence the way NDEs are reported and interpreted. Factors such as social desirability bias, the influence of media or popular culture, and the expectations of researchers or interviewers can impact the narratives and descriptions of NDEs. These biases can influence the consistency and accuracy of reported accounts.

Experimenter bias can influence the framing of questions, data collection methods, and interpretations of findings in NDE research. Researchers' own beliefs, expectations, and preconceptions about NDEs can unintentionally influence the research process, potentially leading to biased results. Efforts to minimize experimenter bias through rigorous research designs and blind data analysis techniques are important in NDE research.